NFL (A

(A Fascinating Book Containing NFL Facts, Trivia, Images & Memory Recall Quiz: Suitable for Adults & Children)

By

Matthew Harper

Image Courtesy of Simanek

For legal reasons we are obliged to state the following:

Hi and a very warm welcome to "NFL (American Football)".

I'm one of those people who loves to hear about extraordinary facts or trivia about anything. They seem to be one of the few things my memory can actually recall. I'm not sure if it's to do with the shock or the "WoW" factor but for some reason my brain seems to store at least some of it for a later date.

I've always been a great believer in that whatever the subject, if a good teacher can inspire you and hold your attention, then you'll learn! Now I'm not a teacher but the system I've used in previous publications on Amazon seems to work well, particularly with children.

This edition includes a selection of those "WoW" facts combined with some pretty awesome pictures, if I say so myself! At the end there is a short "True or False" quiz to check memory recall and to help cement some of the information included in the book. Don't worry though, it's a bit of fun but at the same time, it helps to check your understanding.

Please note that if you're an expert on this subject then you may not find anything new here. If however you enjoy hearing sensational and extraordinary trivia and you like looking at some great pictures then I think you'll love it.

Matt.

I thought that before we get down to some of those amazing football facts, we might begin with some snapshots, just to get the juices flowing..........

JOE MONTANA

Image Courtesy of cliff1066™

JIM BROWN

image Courtesy of Officer Phil

WALTER PAYTON

Image Courtesy of KoryeLogan

PEYTON MANNING

BARRY SANDERS

REGGIE WHITE

Image Courtesy of David Wilson

JOHNNY UNITAS

Image Courtesy of Joel Kaufman

DAN MARINO

DEACON JONES

Image Courtesy of zennie62

TOM BRADY

Image Courtesy of Jeffrey Beall

Okay, that's it for the warm up, let's get on with the game......

Image Courtesy of snydergd

Did you know that NFL cheerleaders are paid around $50 to $75 per game, but it can cost more than that to complete their required beauty treatments for each game?

Image Courtesy of Mike Morbeck

Did you know that until recently, the longest field goal ever recorded was 63 yards by Tom Dempsey, in 1970? Astonishing when you consider that Dempsey was born without any toes on his right foot!

An NFL Films shot of the right foot of Tom Dempsey

Did you know that between 1921 & 1923, the Canton Bulldogs went 25 continuous games without defeat? This NFL record still stands today.

Did you know that the NFL only decided to place the goalposts at the back of the end zone in 1974?

Image Courtesy of hoyasmeg

Did you know that Deion Sanders, in 1989, was the only player to hit a major league home run and score an NFL touchdown in the same week? He is also the only man to have played in both a Super Bowl and a World Series!

Image Courtesy of Jim Accordino

Did you know that the New York Giants are the only team to win Super Bowls in four different decades, (1986, 1990, 2007 & 2011)?

Image Courtesy of Randy Levine

Did you know that the sport was originally played with a round ball but the league wanted to promote passing skills and so by 1934, the ball had evolved to the shape you see today?

Did you know that Tony Dorsett holds the NFL record for the longest run from scrimmage, to complete a 99-yard touchdown?

Image Courtesy of OPEN Sports

Did you know that American Football was adapted from the English games of rugby and soccer and became popular with American students in the late 1800s?

William "Pudge" Heffelfinger

Did you know that if by some miracle every NFL game finished in a tie, the Super Bowl playoffs would be decided by the simple flip of a coin?

Image Courtesy of jeff_golden

Did you know that during a typical 3 hour game, the ball is only in play for around 11 minutes? The remaining time is used showing advertisements, line ups, huddles and replays.

Image Courtesy of Jeffrey Beall

Did you know that the "Miami Dolphins" were the first team to play at 3 consecutive Super Bowls?

Did you know that the home team must, under NFL rules, provide a minimum of 24 footballs for each game played?

Image Courtesy of PixelFish

Did you also know that the NFL insists that football fields must be built facing north/south, or in the shade, so the sun does not disrupt play?

Image Courtesy of farlane

Did you know that Walter Camp, (player, coach & sports writer), is considered the "Father of American Football"? He was also highly influential in helping to develop the rules of the game.

Did you know that the name "Baltimore Ravens" originates from Edgar Alan Poe's famous poem, "The Raven", as Poe spent much of his time there and is buried in Baltimore?

Edgar Allan Poe

Did you know that the NFL record for the longest losing streak in a single season goes to the "Detroit Lions"? They lost 16 games!

Image Courtesy of Dave Hogg

Did you know that Wilson Sporting Goods, (based in Chicago, Illinois), manufacture over 2 million assorted footballs per year and have officially supplied the NFL since 1941?

Image Courtesy of Torsten Bolten

Did you know that the NFL earns over $9 billion per year of which around $1 billion is pure profit?

Image Courtesy of DonkeyHotey

Did you know that the 27th Super Bowl was transferred from Sun Devil Stadium in Arizona to the Rose Bowl in California due to controversy over Arizona's refusal to recognise a new federal holiday, Martin Luther King, Jr. Day?

Image Courtesy of Bobak Ha'Eri

Did you know that the "Green Bay Packers" are the only major-league professional sports team in the U.S.A. who are community-owned and non-profit making?

Image Courtesy of Mike Morbeck

Did you know that the "Tampa Bay Buccaneers" became the first team in the NFL (1976) to lose every one of their 14-games season without even tying?

Image Courtesy of Bizkit99

Did you know that during a typical broadcast NFL game, cheerleaders appear on TV for an average of 3 seconds while coaches and referees receive around 7% broadcast time?

Did you know that the NFL has 32 teams, each team being worth an average of $1 billion? Major League Baseball on the other hand, has 30 teams which only have an average team value of $523 million.

Image Courtesy of Scott Ableman

Did you know that fans of the "Seattle Seahawks" hold the Guinness World Record for being the loudest crowd at a sporting event?

Image Courtesy of UW Dawgs

Did you know that there are 6 NFL teams who don't employ cheerleaders? These are the Bears, Browns, Lions, Giants, Steelers and the Packers?

Image Courtesy of Jason Pero

Did you know that player's names were not introduced on to the back of their jerseys until the 1960s?

Image Courtesy of Ken Lund

Did you know that currently, (according to Forbes), the "Dallas Cowboys" are the 5th most valuable team in the world worth an estimated $2.3 billion? First is "Real Madrid" (soccer) valued at a cool $3.44 billion.

Image Courtesy of Wright Way Photography

Did you know that while players for the National Basketball Association earn around $4 million, NFL players only average around $1.5 million salary? Still, not a bad way to make a living!

Image Courtesy of cliff1066™

Did you know that it takes around 3,000 cattle to produce enough football leather for a year of NFL tournaments?

Did you know that the city of Miami has hosted the most Super Bowls, which currently stands at 10?

Image Courtesy of Averette

Did you know that the Super Bowl weekend is the second largest grilling weekend in the U.S. only surpassed by 4th July celebrations?

Image Courtesy of Fifth World Art

Did you know that the oldest NFL stadium still in use is Chicago's "Soldier Field"?

Image Courtesy of Joon Han

Did you know that California currently has the largest supply of NFL teams, closely followed by Florida, then New York?

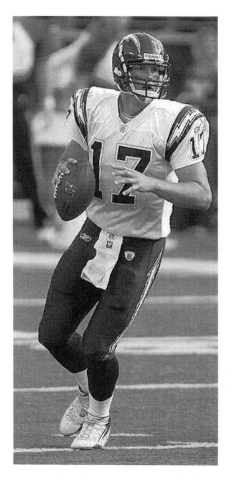

Image Courtesy of Keith Allison

Did you know that many NFL teams have won two consecutive championships, but only the Pittsburgh Steelers have won two consecutive championships more than once?

Image Courtesy of SteelCityHobbies

Did you know that the wearing of helmets only became mandatory in 1939 for all American football players?

Image Courtesy of LandRover164

Did you know that NFL players can be fined up to $5000, for giving game balls to fans?

Image Courtesy of gfairchild

Did you know that the Buffalo Bills are the only team to have lost the Super Bowl for four consecutive years?

Image Courtesy of Dougtone

Did you know that on Super Bowl Sunday, pizza sales are higher than on any other day of the year?

Image Courtesy of hectorir

Did you also know that unsurprisingly, pizza delivery drivers have more accidents on Super Bowl Sunday than any other day of the year?

Image Courtesy of liftarn

Did you know that 78% of NFL professional players are bankrupt within 2 years of retiring from football?

Imager Courtesy of danielmoyle

Did you know that players who frequently carry or catch the ball, wear very tight pants to prevent other players grabbing them when running?

Image Courtesy of Monica's Dad

Did you know that the first, black professional American footballer was Charles Follis in 1904?

Did you know that American footballs are eleven inches long (27.940cm), have a circumference of 28 inches (71.120cm) & weigh between 14 and 15 ounces (397-425 grams approx)?

Image Courtesy of RonAlmog

Did you know that even though the NFL generates billions of dollars in revenue, it pays no taxes? The IRS considers it to be a "non-profit organization"!

Image Courtesy of gruntzooki

Did you know that recent studies showed the average lifespan of an NFL player to be approximately 20 years less than the rest of the population?

Image Courtesy of Erik Daniel Drost

Did you know that Super Bowl 1 was played on January 15, 1967? Although the game was broadcast by 2 television networks, all recordings were wiped leaving no footage of this historical moment.

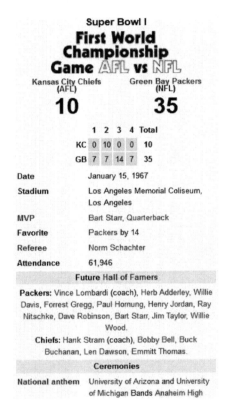

Super Bowl I
First World Championship Game AFL vs NFL

Kansas City Chiefs (AFL) Green Bay Packers (NFL)

10   35

	1	2	3	4	Total
KC	0	10	0	0	10
GB	7	7	14	7	35

Date	January 15, 1967
Stadium	Los Angeles Memorial Coliseum, Los Angeles
MVP	Bart Starr, Quarterback
Favorite	Packers by 14
Referee	Norm Schachter
Attendance	61,946

Future Hall of Famers

Packers: Vince Lombardi (coach), Herb Adderley, Willie Davis, Forrest Gregg, Paul Hornung, Henry Jordan, Ray Nitschke, Dave Robinson, Bart Starr, Jim Taylor, Willie Wood.

Chiefs: Hank Stram (coach), Bobby Bell, Buck Buchanan, Len Dawson, Emmitt Thomas.

Ceremonies

National anthem	University of Arizona and University of Michigan Bands Anaheim High

Image Courtesy of wikipedia.org

Did you know that Darrell Ray Green was one of the fastest cornerbacks in NFL history? One of his rituals before each game was to put "Tootsie Rolls" into his sock claiming that the candy gave him extra speed!

Image Courtesy of oskay

Did you know that Terry Bradshaw is the only former NFL player to date who, in 2001, received a star on the "Hollywood Walk of Fame"?

Did you know that Tony Dungy was the first African American head coach to win a Super Bowl?

That's about it for the football trivia for now. I'd like to finish this publication with TEN "True or False" questions based on what you've just read. It should help you to really cement the information and to test your memory recall!

....

....

DON'T FORGET TO KEEP YOUR SCORE: THERE'S 1 POINT FOR EACH OF THE FIRST 9 QUESTIONS AND 5 POINTS FOR THE BONUS QUESTION GIVING A TOTAL OF 14 POINTS ....

1.

TRUE or FALSE: Between 1921 & 1923, the Canton Bulldogs went 25 continuous games without defeat.

TRUE.

2.

TRUE or FALSE: Tony Dorsett holds the NFL record for the longest run from scrimmage, to complete a 199-yard touchdown.

FALSE

Tony Dorsett holds the NFL record for the longest run from scrimmage, to complete a **99-yard** touchdown.

3.

TRUE or FALSE: Walter Camp, (player, coach & sports writer), is considered the "Father of American Football".

TRUE

4.

TRUE or FALSE: The "Seattle Sealions" hold the Guinness
World Record for being the loudest crowd at a sporting event.

FALSE

The "Seattle **SeaHAWKS**" hold the Guinness World Record for being the loudest crowd at a sporting event.

5.

TRUE or FALSE: There are 6 NFL teams who don't employ cheerleaders.

TRUE

6.

TRUE or FALSE: It takes around 3,000 pigs to produce enough football leather for a year of NFL tournaments..

FALSE

It takes around 3,000 **CATTLE** to produce enough football
leather for a year of NFL tournaments.

7.

TRUE or FALSE: The wearing of helmets only became mandatory in 1939 for all American football players.

TRUE

8.

TRUE or FALSE: 78% of NFL professional players are bankrupt within 2 years of retiring from football.

TRUE

9.

TRUE or FALSE: The first, black professional American footballer was Charles Follis in 1944.

FALSE

The first, black professional American footballer was Charles Follis in **1904**.

10.

BONUS ROUND WORTH 5 POINTS

TRUE or FALSE: Larry Bradshaw is the only former NFL player to date who, in 2001, received a star on the "Hollywood Walk of Fame".

FALSE

TERRY Bradshaw is the only former NFL player to date who, in 2001, received a star on the "Hollywood Walk of Fame".

Congratulations, you made it to the end!

I sincerely hope you enjoyed my little NFL project and that you learnt a thing or two. I certainly did when I was doing the research. **No Tax**!

ADD UP YOUR SCORE NOW.

1 point for each of the first 9 correct answers plus 5 points for the bonus round giving a grand total of 14 points.

If you genuinely achieved 14 points then you are indeed an

"NFL MASTER".

8 to 13 points proves you are an **"NFL LEGEND"**.

4 to 7 points shows you are an **"NFL ENTHUSIAST"**.

0 to 3 points shows you are an **"NFL ADMIRER"**.

NICE WORK!

Matt.

Thank you once again for choosing this publication. If you enjoyed it then please let me know using the Customer Review Section through Amazon.

If you would like to read more of my work then simply type in my name using the Amazon Search Box and hopefully you'll find something else that "takes your fancy" or go directly to my website printed below.

Until we meet again,

Matthew Harper

www.matthewharper.info

Image Courtesy of Simanek

Made in the USA
Middletown, DE
08 December 2015